Title: Swimming with sea
R.L.: 4.5
PTS: 0.5
TST: 132012

Flippers and Fins ™

Swimming with Sea Turtles

Miriam Coleman

PowerKiDS press™

New York

Published in 2010 by The Rosen Publishing Group, Inc.
29 East 21st Street, New York, NY 10010

First Edition

Editor: Joanne Randolph
Book Design: Greg Tucker
Photo Researcher: Jessica Gerweck

Photo Credits: Cover, p. 5 Jeff Hunter/Getty Images; p. 7 George Grall/Getty Images; p. 9 © Michele Westmorland/Corbis; p. 11 Georgette Douwma/Getty Images; p. 13 © Stephen Frink/Corbis; p. 15 Sami Sarkis/Getty Images; p. 17 © Reinhard Dirscherl/age fotostock; p. 19 © Kevin Schafer/Corbis; p. 21 Reinhard Dirscherl/Getty Images.

Library of Congress Cataloging-in-Publication Data

Coleman, Miriam.
    Swimming with sea turtles / Miriam Coleman. — 1st ed.
        p. cm. — (Flippers and fins)
    Includes index.
    ISBN 978-1-4042-8093-9 (library binding) — ISBN 978-1-4358-3243-5 (pbk.) —
ISBN 978-1-4358-3244-2 (6-pack)
    1. Sea turtles—Juvenile literature. I. Title.
    QL666.C536C64 2010
    597.92'8—dc22
                                    2008053810

Manufactured in the United States of America

Contents

About the Sea Turtle   4

Kinds of Sea Turtles   6

Where Sea Turtles Live   8

Turtle Shells   10

All About the Flippers   12

Living in the Sea   14

Sea Turtle Snacks   16

Coming Ashore   18

Baby Turtles   20

Save the Sea Turtles   22

Glossary   23

Index   24

Web Sites   24

About the Sea Turtle

Nesting on a dark beach, where the only light comes from the Moon, sea turtles look like giant stones. Some sea turtles can grow to be almost as large as a car. Their big, hard shells make them **clumsy** on land, but sea turtles swim easily through the water. They can swim a very long way, too.

Sea turtles have been around for a long time. They have wandered the seas since before the time of the dinosaurs. Sea turtles are **reptiles**, just like lizards and snakes. Although sea turtles are born on land, they spend their lives in the ocean.

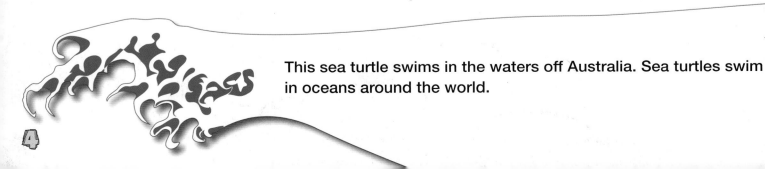

This sea turtle swims in the waters off Australia. Sea turtles swim in oceans around the world.

Kinds of Sea Turtles

There are eight different species, or types, of sea turtles. The different species range in color from green to yellow to reddish brown to black. Seven of these species belong to the same sea turtle family.

The leatherback sea turtle is in a family all by itself. The leatherback is the largest sea turtle. Leatherback turtles are generally 4 to 6 feet (1–2 m) long. A leatherback turtle was once found that weighed more than 2,000 pounds (900 kg)!

The Kemp's ridley and olive ridley sea turtles are the smallest species. They grow to be only about 22 to 30 inches (55–76 cm) long.

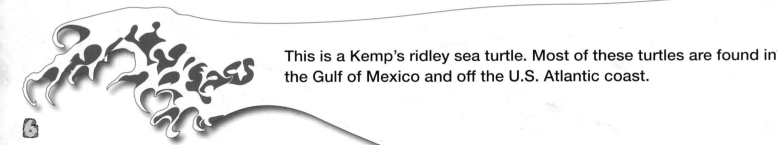

This is a Kemp's ridley sea turtle. Most of these turtles are found in the Gulf of Mexico and off the U.S. Atlantic coast.

Where Sea Turtles Live

Sea turtles live all over the world, from Alaska to Brazil. Most live in warm and **temperate** water, but leatherbacks also travel into very cold water. Most sea turtles live in **shallow** water near the shore or in bays, **lagoons**, and **estuaries**. The hawksbill sea turtle, for example, lives near **coral reefs** and rocky areas along the coast.

Sea turtles migrate, or travel, a long way between the places where they live and eat and the beaches where they lay their eggs. Leatherbacks can travel over 3,000 miles (4,800 km) to reach their nesting places.

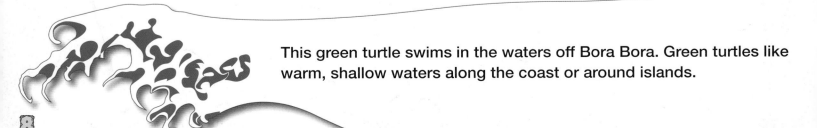

This green turtle swims in the waters off Bora Bora. Green turtles like warm, shallow waters along the coast or around islands.

Turtle Shells

All turtles have shells to **protect** their bodies. Most turtles can pull their heads and limbs in, but sea turtles cannot. Instead, sea turtle shells are shaped to help them swim better.

The top part of a turtle's shell is called the carapace. The lower part is called the castron. All turtle shells have an inner part made of bony plates. Most sea turtles have hard plates called scutes over these bony plates. Scutes are made of keratin, the same type of matter that forms people's fingernails and animals' horns.

Leatherbacks do not have scutes. Instead, their shells are covered with a thick, oily skin.

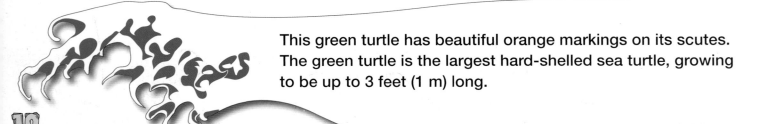

This green turtle has beautiful orange markings on its scutes. The green turtle is the largest hard-shelled sea turtle, growing to be up to 3 feet (1 m) long.

All About the Flippers

Sea turtles have two sets of flippers. Hidden inside each flipper, a turtle has bony parts, which are like human fingers and toes. All sea turtles except leatherbacks have one or two claws at the ends of their flippers.

A sea turtle's front flippers are long and powerful. The sea turtle moves its front flippers like wings in order to swim. Its back flippers are smaller. Sea turtles use their back flippers to change direction and sometimes to paddle. When sea turtles are on land, they can use their flippers to crawl and dig in the sand. Some turtles use their front flippers to dig nests on land, and some use their back flippers.

This is a loggerhead turtle. Loggerheads must have strong flippers since they swim for hundreds or even thousands of miles (km) between feeding and nesting places.

Sea turtles breathe air, just as people do. However, sea turtles have a very slow metabolism. Metabolism is how fast a body uses its energy. This means that they need less **oxygen** to live than people do. This lets them stay underwater for a very long time. Most sea turtles can stay underwater for a few hours, but black sea turtles can hide under the mud on the ocean floor all winter long!

Sea turtles also have a special way of getting freshwater from the salty ocean. As the turtles take seawater into their bodies, a **gland** near the eyes takes in all the salt from the water. Sea turtles then "cry" the salt out through their eyes.

A green turtle, like this one, can stay underwater for up to 5 hours at a time. This one swims to the top of the water to breathe.

Sea Turtle Snacks

Different species of sea turtles eat different foods. Their jaws are shaped differently so that they can better eat their favorite meals.

Loggerhead and ridley turtles have strong jaws to crush the shells of crabs and **mollusks**. Hawksbill turtles have pointy jaws to pull animals out of tight spaces in coral reefs. They like to eat sponges, shrimp, and squid. Leatherbacks have jaws that are good for eating soft animals like jellyfish.

Other sea turtles are herbivores, which means they eat only plants. Green turtles have sawlike jaws, which are good for cutting through turtle grasses and algae.

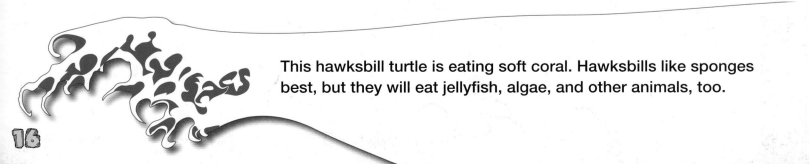

This hawksbill turtle is eating soft coral. Hawksbills like sponges best, but they will eat jellyfish, algae, and other animals, too.

Coming Ashore

When a mother turtle is ready to lay eggs, she crawls up out of the water and onto a beach. This is the only time a sea turtle leaves the sea. Turtles are slow and clumsy on land, so it is not a safe trip for them.

Mother sea turtles may swim a very long way to get to a nesting place. Some turtles, such as the Kemp's ridley and olive ridley turtles, come ashore in large groups. This is called the arribada, or arrival.

When the mother reaches the beach, she digs a deep hole in the sand with her flippers. She lays her eggs in the hole. Then she covers the eggs with sand to hide them from animals. When she is done, the mother hurries back to the sea for safety.

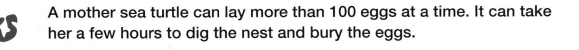

A mother sea turtle can lay more than 100 eggs at a time. It can take her a few hours to dig the nest and bury the eggs.

Baby Turtles

Baby sea turtles grow inside their eggs for 45 to 70 days. When it is time to **hatch**, the turtles use their beaks to cut through the eggshells. Once the babies have hatched, they dig themselves out of the nest. This can take four or five days. While the babies dig, the shells on their bodies become harder.

Baby sea turtles will leave their nests only at night, when fewer animals are out to hunt them. Then they must run to the sea as quickly as possible so they are not eaten. Once they reach the sea, baby sea turtles swim toward deeper, safer waters.

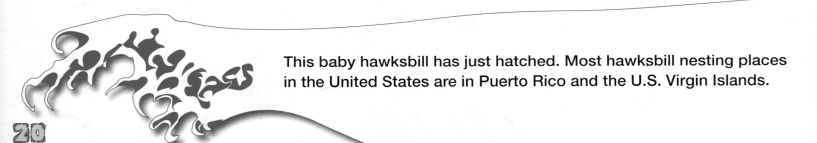

This baby hawksbill has just hatched. Most hawksbill nesting places in the United States are in Puerto Rico and the U.S. Virgin Islands.

Save the Sea Turtles

People have hunted sea turtles for thousands of years. They cook the turtles in soups. They make combs out of the turtles' shells. Sea turtles also get caught by mistake in nets that are meant for shrimp. All sea turtle species are now in danger of becoming extinct, or disappearing forever. Many countries have made it illegal to hunt these creatures.

People also harm sea turtles by polluting the waters that turtles live in and by building homes on the beaches where turtles lay their eggs. Without safe nesting places, new turtles cannot be born. What can you do to help?

Glossary

clumsy (KLUM-zee) Moving without skill or grace.

coral reefs (KOR-ul REEFS) Underwater hills of coral, which is hard matter made up of the bones of tiny sea animals.

estuaries (ES-choo-wer-eez) Areas of water where ocean tides meet rivers.

gland (GLAND) A part of the body that produces something to help the body do something.

hatch (HACH) To break out of an egg.

lagoons (luh-GOONZ) Shallow ponds or channels that are near a larger body of water.

mollusks (MAH-lusks) Animals without backbones that have soft bodies and, often, shells.

oxygen (OK-sih-jen) A gas that people and animals need to breathe.

protect (pruh-TEKT) To keep safe.

reptiles (REP-tylz) Cold-blooded animals with lungs and scales.

shallow (SHA-loh) Not deep.

temperate (TEM-puh-rut) Not too hot or too cold.

Index

B
beach(es), 4, 8, 18, 22
beaks, 20
bodies, 10, 14, 20

C
car, 4
coral reefs, 8, 16

D
dinosaurs, 4

E
estuaries, 8

G
gland, 14

L
lagoons, 8
land, 4, 12, 18
leatherback(s), 6, 8, 10, 12, 16
light, 4
lizards, 4

M
mollusks, 16
Moon, 4

O
oxygen, 14

R
reptiles, 4

S
sea(s), 4, 18, 20
shells, 4, 10, 16, 20, 22
snakes, 4
stones, 4

W
water(s), 4, 8, 14, 18, 20, 22

Web Sites

Due to the changing nature of Internet links, PowerKids Press has developed an online list of Web sites related to the subject of this book. This site is updated regularly. Please use this link to access the list:

www.powerkidslinks.com/ffin/seaturtle/